D0975303

ALSO BY

ANNA QUINDLEN

Loud and Clear

Blessings

A Short Guide to a Happy Life

How Reading Changed My Life

Black and Blue

One True Thing

Object Lessons

Living Out Loud

Thinking Out Loud

BOOKS FOR

CHILDREN

The Tree That Came to Stay

Happily Ever After

Being Perfect

Being Perfect

ANNA QUINDLEN

Random House
New York

Published in the United States by Random House,
an imprint of The Random House Publishing Group,
a division of Random House, Inc., New York.

Photo credits are located on page 51.

RANDOM HOUSE and colophon are registered
trademarks of Random House, Inc.

ISBN: 0-375-50549-0

Printed in the United States of America on acid-free paper
Random House website address: www.atrandom.com

2 4 6 8 9 7 5 3 1

FIRST EDITION

Book design by Barbara M. Bachman

For Kate Medina,

the perfect editor

Being Perfect

When I try to recall the girl I was decades ago, at my high school graduation, I seem to have as much in common with her as I do with any stranger I might pass in the doorway of a Starbucks or in the aisle of an airplane. I cannot remember exactly what she wore, or how she felt, or what she said, or ate, or read. But I can tell you this about her without question: She was perfect.

Let me be very clear about what I mean by that. I mean that I got up every day and tried

to be perfect in every possible way. If there was a test to be taken, I had studied for it; if there was a paper to be written, it was done. I smiled at everyone in the hallways because it was important to be friendly, and I made fun of them behind their backs because it was important to be witty. And I edited the newspaper and cheered at pep rallies and emoted for the literary magazine and rode on the back of a convertible at the homecoming game and if anyone had ever stopped and asked me why I did those things—well, I'm not sure that I could have said why. But in hindsight I can say that I did them to be perfect, in every possible way.

Being perfect was hard work, and the hell of it was, the rules kept changing. So that

NEMA

while I arrived at college in 1970 with a trunk full of perfect pleated kilts and perfect monogrammed sweaters, by Christmas vacation I had another perfect uniform: overalls, turtlenecks, clogs, and the perfect New York City college affect, part hypercerebral, part ennui. This was very hard work indeed. I had read neither Sartre nor Sappho, and the closest I ever came to being bored and above it all was falling asleep. And, finally, it was harder to become perfect because I realized at Barnard, a place populated largely by terrifyingly well-read women who all seemed to be elevating intellectual perfection to a high art, that I was not the smartest girl in the world. And eventually being perfect became like carrying a backpack filled with bricks every single day.

And oh, how I wanted to lay my burden down.

So if this sounds in any way familiar to you, if you have been trying to be perfect, too, then perhaps today is the day to put down that backpack before you develop permanent curvature of the spirit. Trying to be perfect may be inevitable for people who are smart and ambitious and interested in the world and in its good opinion. But at one level it's too hard, and at another, it's too cheap and easy. Because all it really requires of you, mainly, is to read the zeitgeist of wherever and whenever you happen to be and to assume the masks necessary to be the best at whatever the zeitgeist dictates or requires. Those requirements shape-shift, sure, but when you're clever you

IXL
FILE
DIRECTORY

can read them and come up with the imitation necessary.

But nothing important, or meaningful, or beautiful, or interesting, or great, ever came out of imitations. What is really hard, and really amazing, is giving up on being perfect and beginning the work of becoming yourself.

More difficult because there is no zeitgeist to read, no template to follow, no mask to wear. Terrifying, actually, because it requires you to set aside what your friends expect, what your family and your co-workers demand, what your acquaintances require, to set aside the messages this culture sends, through its advertising, its entertainment, its disdain, and its disapproval, about how you should behave.

Set aside the old traditional notion of

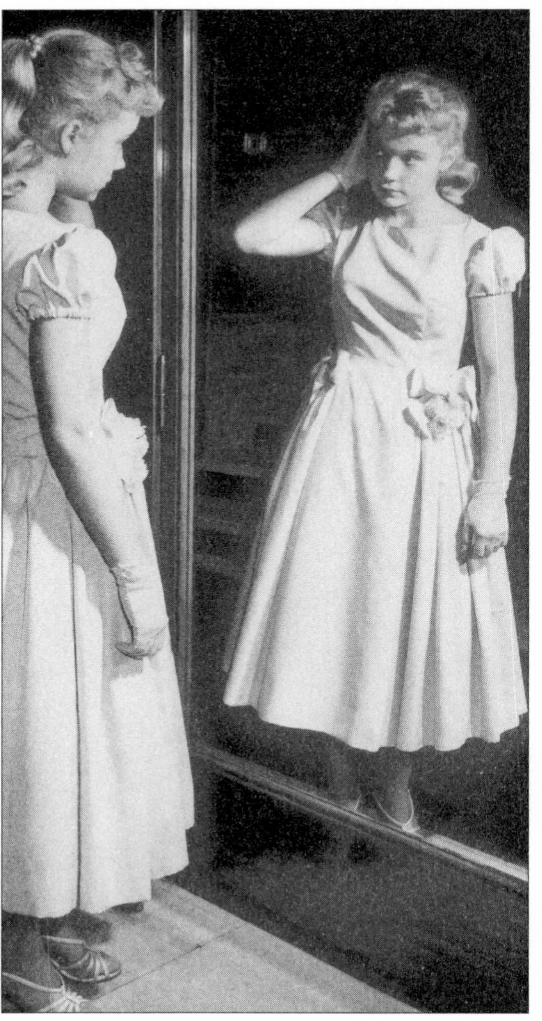

female as nurturer and male as leader; set aside, too, the new traditional notion of female as superwoman and male as oppressor. Begin with that most frightening of all things, a clean slate. And then look, every day, at the choices you are making, and when you ask yourself why you are making them, find this answer: Because they are what I want, or wish for. Because they reflect who and what I am.

This is the hard work of life in the world, to acknowledge within yourself the introvert, the clown, the artist, the homebody, the goofball, the thinker. Look inside. That way lies dancing to the melodies spun out by your own heart.

It would seem as though this is the perfect moment in history to live with imperfection,

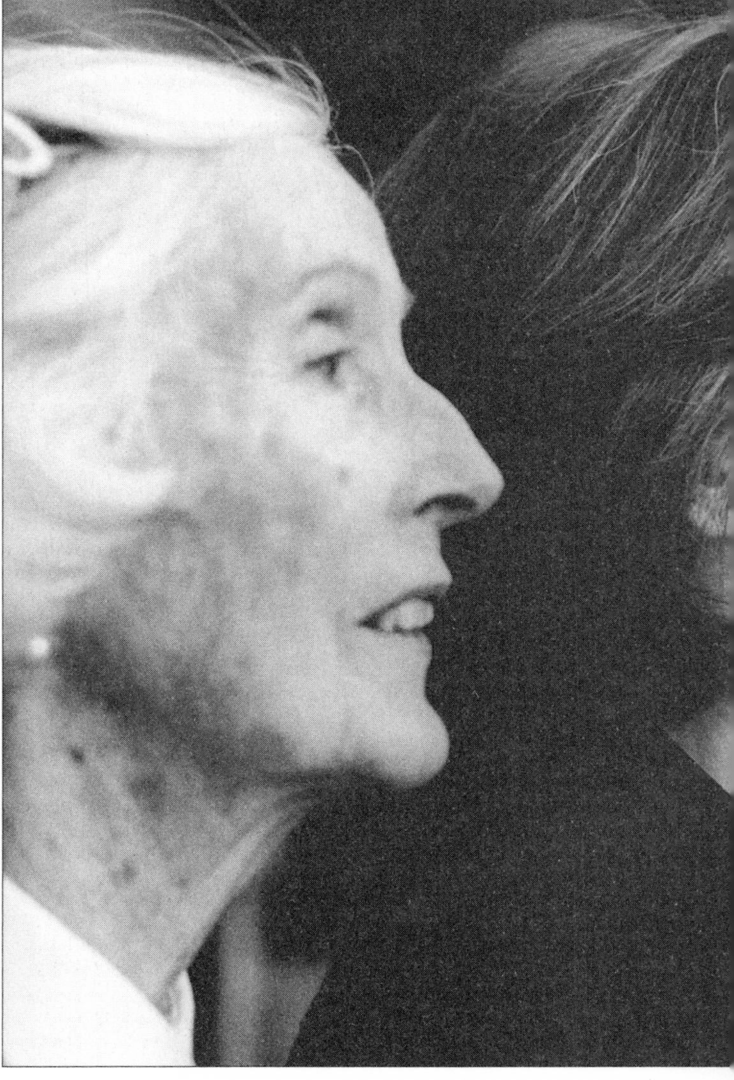

to embrace variety and leave conformity on the assembly lines. The strictures that once defined human behavior have relaxed in many ways. Gay men and lesbians are able to reveal themselves to those they love. Different complexions, origins, and languages have become the norm, not the exception. The eccentric and the unusual have more room to grow unapologetically, and even to prosper. Sometimes I think the key to understanding how far we've moved over my lifetime is small and sartorial. Fewer occasions require ties. A girdle is no longer de rigueur. This is a more polymorphous world than the one in which I grew up. There is very little left worth staring at except in admiration.

And yet occasionally the old ghosts rise

and remind us that the traditional ways are tenacious in reasserting themselves. When the president of Duke University commissioned a study on the status of women at the school, the results, released in 2003, were astonishing. Female undergraduates talked of a culture at the college of "effortless perfection," in which they were expected to be attractive, well-dressed, in great shape, and academically able.

I was mesmerized by that phrase: effortless perfection. Obviously it is an oxymoron. Even the illusion of perfection requires an enormous amount of work. I can tell you that by the end of a day of trying to be perfect I was always as exhausted as if I'd done the whole thing at a fast clip in running shoes. There's some muscle group around your

shoulders that seizes up during the perfection dance and doesn't let go until you are asleep, or alone. Or maybe it never really lets go at all.

But the more disconcerting thing about the notion of effortless perfection is that effort is the point of the exercise, of any exercise at all, from push-ups to poetry. Oh, there are times when I wish the 350-page text of a novel would just miraculously appear, without typos, run-on sentences, or the telltale smell of creative desperation. But what exactly would that be, a novel, or a paper, or a poem, or even a legal brief or a syllabus, that appears magically from the lamp of "I wish"? Perhaps we will find out someday soon, with the rise of the computer. Perhaps we will be able to read

something over which a real person has not sweated and sworn; perhaps we will find out precisely what the thing lacks that only effort can confer. Is it soul? Passion? Vivid reality? If I had to guess, I would say it would be all three.

The computer analogy is apt, I think, because perfection implies a combination of rote and bloodlessness that is essentially made for machines, not men and women. It is also bound to alienate others. "Perfection irritates as well as it attracts," the writer Louis Auchincloss, who wrote of the careful facades in the world of old money, once said. But it torments, too, both those who are trying to attain it and those who feel they never can. The perfect mother (the toughest of all the

ideals to imagine!) makes other women feel like failures simply by showing up and showing off. The perfect student can never step outside the safe box of the right answer, can never take a flyer on the honorable failure that may be more compelling than the safe paper that gets an A. What perfection requires is a kind of lockstep. Look at that word; imagine it in your mind's eye, the forced march of the fearful, the physical opposite of the skip and the jump. Doesn't it sound like something to avoid at all costs?

Lockstep is easier, but there's another reason why you cannot succumb to it. Because nothing great or even good ever came of it. Sometimes I meet young writers, and I like to share with them the overwhelming feeling I have about our work, the feeling that every story has already been told. Once you've read *Anna Karenina, Bleak House, The Sound and the Fury, To Kill a Mockingbird,* and *A Wrinkle in Time,* you understand that there is really no reason ever to write another novel. Except that each writer brings to the table, if she will let herself, something that no one else in the history of time ever has. That is her own personality, her own voice. If she is doing Fitzgerald imitations, she can stay home. If she is giving readers what she thinks they want instead of what she is, she should stop typing.

But if her books reflect her character, the authentic shape of her life and her mind, then she may well be giving readers a new and wonderful gift. Giving it to herself, too.

And that is true of music and art and teaching and medicine. Someone sent me a T-shirt once that read WELL-BEHAVED WOMEN DON'T MAKE HISTORY. They don't make good lawyers, either, or businesswomen. Perfection is static, even boring. Imitations are redundant. Your true unvarnished self is what is wanted.

This is especially true in one essential walk of life. Sometime in the future, if you are young, you may want to be a parent. You will convince yourself that you will be a better parent than your parents and their parents have been. But being a good parent is not generational, it is deeply personal, and it all comes down to this: If you can bring to your children the self that you truly are, as opposed to some amalgam of manners and mannerisms, expectations and fears that you have acquired as a carapace along the way, you will be able to teach them by example not to be terrorized by the narrow and parsimonious expectations of the world, a world that often likes to color within the lines when a spray of paint, a scribble of crayon, would be much more satisfying.

For the sake of those children, you must look backward instead of ahead, to remember yourself from your own childhood days, when you were younger and rougher and wilder, more scrawl than straight line. Remember all of yourself, the flaws as well as the many strengths. Pursuing perfection makes you unforgiving of the faults of others. As Carl Jung once said, "If people can be educated to

see the lowly side of their own natures, it may be hoped that they will also learn to understand and to love their fellow men better. A little less hypocrisy and a little more tolerance towards oneself can only have good results in respect for our neighbor; for we are all too prone to transfer to our fellows the injustice and violence we inflict upon our own natures."

Most of the time when we're giving people advice we suggest that they take up something or other: the challenge of the future, the work of a new century. But I don't really know what the challenge of the future will be, and I'm still working on the work of a new century. I'm more comfortable advising people to give up. Give up the nonsensical and

punishing quest for perfection that dogs too many of us through too much of our lives. It is a quest that causes us to doubt and denigrate ourselves, our true selves, our quirks and foibles and great heroic leaps into the unknown. Much of what we were at five or six is what we wind up wishing we could be at fifty or sixty. And that's bad enough.

But this is worse: Someday, sometime, you will be sitting somewhere. A berm overlooking a pond in Vermont. The lip of the Grand Canyon at sunset. A seat on the subway. And something bad will have happened: You will have lost someone you loved, or failed at something at which you badly wanted to succeed.

And sitting there, you will fall into the

center of yourself. You will look for some core to sustain you. And if you have been perfect all your life and have managed to meet all the expectations of your family, your friends, your community, your society, chances are excellent that there will be a black hole where that core ought to be.

I don't want anyone I know to take that terrible chance. And the only way to avoid it is to listen to that small voice inside you that tells you to make mischief, to have fun, to be contrarian, to go another way. George Eliot wrote, "It is never too late to be what you might have been." It is never too early, either. Take it from someone who has left the backpack full of bricks far behind, and every day feels light as a feather.

Photo Credits

Cover and 2: Owen Franken/Corbis
4–5: Hulton Archive/Getty Images
7: Hulton Archive/Getty Images
8–9: Bettmann/Corbis
10: Bettmann/Corbis
13: Taxi/Getty Images
14: Hulton Archive/Getty Images
16–17: Hulton Archive/Getty Images
18: Echos/nonstøck
20–21: Photodisc Red/Getty Images
22: © Minnesota Historical Society/Corbis
24–25: Thomas B. Windholz/Private Collection
27: Hulton Archive/Getty Images
28: Henri Silberman/nonstøck
30–31: Hulton Archive/Getty Images
33: Hulton Archive/Getty Images
34: Rubberball Productions/Getty Images
37: Taxi/Getty Images
38: Hulton Archive/Getty Images
41: Photodisc Blue/Getty Images
42–43: Millennium/nonstøck
45: Taxi/Getty Images
46: Massimo Listri/Corbis
49: Digital Vision/Getty Images

Picture Research:

SARAH LONGACRE

ABOUT THE AUTHOR

ANNA QUINDLEN is the author of four novels—*Blessings, Black and Blue, One True Thing,* and *Object Lessons*—and six nonfiction books: *Being Perfect, Loud and Clear, A Short Guide to a Happy Life, Living Out Loud, Thinking Out Loud,* and *How Reading Changed My Life.* She has also written two children's books: *The Tree That Came to Stay* and *Happily Ever After.* Her *New York Times* column "Public & Private" won the Pulitzer Prize in 1992. Her column now appears every other week in *Newsweek.*

ABOUT THE TYPE

This book is set in Fournier, a typeface named for Pierre Simon Fournier, the youngest son of a French printing family. He started out engraving woodblocks and large capitals, then moved on to fonts of type. In 1736 he began his own foundry and made several important contributions in the field of type design; he is said to have cut 147 alphabets of his own creation. Fournier is probably best remembered as the designer of St. Augustine Ordinaire, a face that served as the model for Monotype's Fournier, which was released in 1925.